IAN PLIMER

THE LITTLE GREEN BOOK

ONE

FOR ANKLE BITERS

Contents

PROFESSOR

IAN PLIMER

Professor Plimer is

Australia's best-known geologist.

He has written more than 130 scientific papers, 13 books

and was an editor of the *Encyclopedia of Geology.*

For his scientific work,

he has a mineral and a spider named after him and has

won awards and prizes all over the world.

Published in 2023 by Connor Court Publishing Pty Ltd
Copyright © Ian Plimer

All rights reserved. No part of this book may be reproduced or transmitted in any form or by any means, electronic or mechanical, including photocopying, recording or by any information storage and retrieval system, without prior permission in writing from the publisher.

Connor Court Publishing Pty Ltd
PO Box 7257
Redland Bay QLD 4165
sales@connorcourt.com
www.connorcourtpublishing.com.au
Phone 0497 900 685
Cover and text design: www.jgd.com.au

ISBN: 9781922815651

Printed in Australia

“

I find it frustrating, as a lay person, to find answers to technical questions. You see gigantic wind turbines appearing all over the country, but there is very little about the practical value of these monstrosities … When will common sense and good science prevail and what happens if it does not fairly soon?

”

Letter from HRH Prince Philip to Professor Plimer, 29th April 2018.

–

This book attempts to answer the questions raised by the late Duke of Edinburgh.

You are what you eat and drink.

For most of time, it was a case of eat or be eaten. 

Today, we now have farms to produce our food and don't have to spend all-day every-day hunting and gathering for food.

Your grandparents might be old fossils. They are not THAT old. Old forests covered the Earth well before dinosaurs appeared.

They dropped leaves and branches. Forests grew by using carbon dioxide, plant food in the air, sunlight, water and soil.

The forests were later covered with sand and mud and then cooked up into coal. The carbon in coal burns, gives out heat and puts carbon dioxide back into the air. It is a fossil fuel.

Other fossil fuels are oil and gas. Dead floating tiny animals accumulated on the sea floor, were covered with sand and mud and were cooked up into oil and gas.

Oil and gas contain carbon that was once in the air. When they are burned, they also give out heat and the carbon dioxide goes back into the air.

Fossil fuels.

Without fossil fuels, it would not be possible for farms to produce foods. Even if the weather was wet and cold for weeks, humans needed to be outside hunting and gathering because food could not be stored in a fridge.

Fridges were invented just over 100 years ago. Half the people in the world still don't have fridges because they don't have electricity. How many fridges do you have in your house?

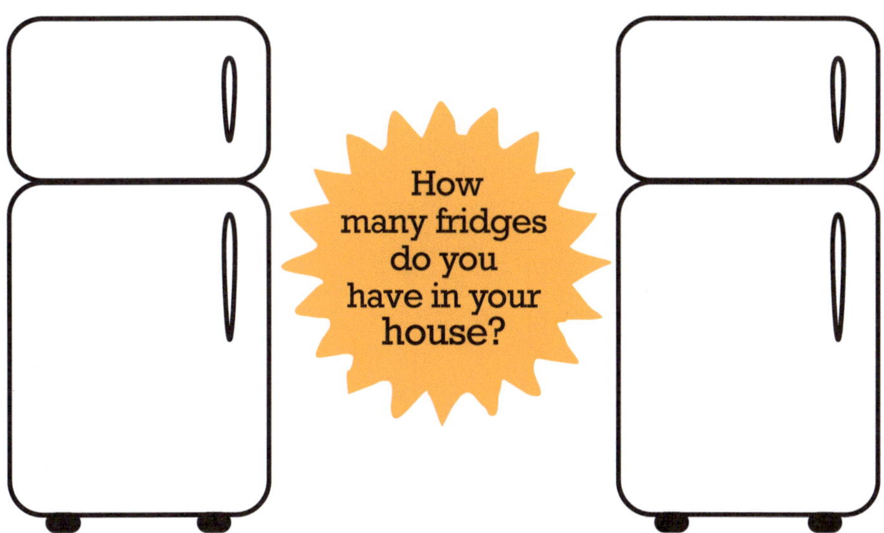

To eat three times a day, we need a farmer three times a day. We may need a doctor or dentist a few times a year, the police every few years and the fire brigade or ambulance once in our life. We need a miner all day every day for the metals, concrete, plastics, fertiliser and energy we use all the time.

Sometimes there was too much food, other times there was no food. More than half of the people in the world have been hungry for days, weeks, months and years at some time in their life. Many people still die from hunger.

Do you like cookies? I do.

The flour, butter and sugar in cookies come from farms. These farms plough fields using fossil fuel-driven tractors, wheat seeds are planted by fossil fuel-driven tractors and tractors are used for weeding and harvesting. Burning fossil fuels makes carbon dioxide.

Wheat grows by using carbon dioxide from the air and water and nutrients from the soil. Crops are fertilised using chemicals made from the air and natural gas.

Sugar comes from sugar cane and butter comes from milk given by cows after eating grass. Both sugar cane and grass are plants.

Wheat, sugar cane, grass and all other plants use carbon dioxide as plant food and put oxygen in the air for you to breathe.

Even green slime uses carbon dioxide as food. Do you eat green slime for food?

The more carbon dioxide in the air, the bigger, better and faster wheat and all other plants grow. If you think carbon dioxide pollutes the planet, then don't eat.

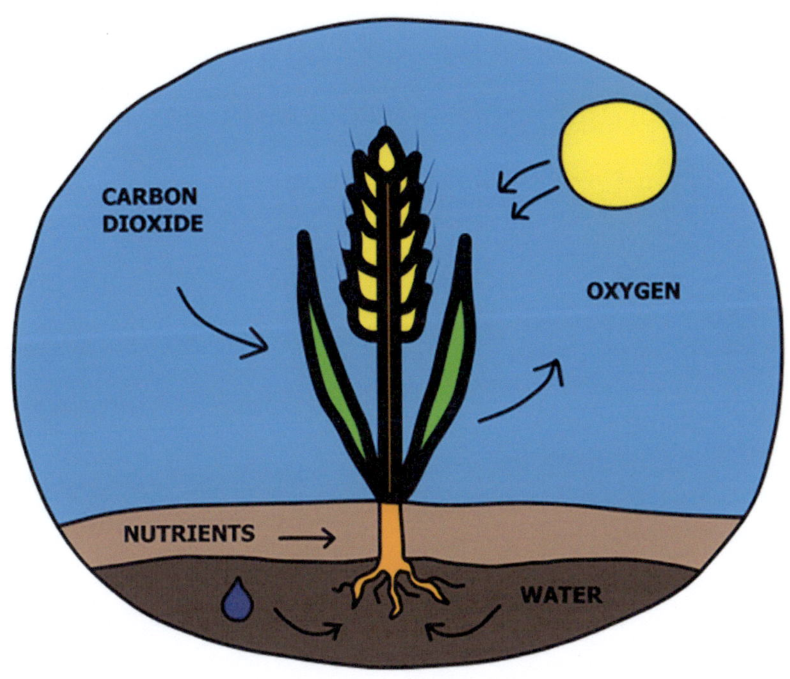

The harvested wheat is taken by fossil fuel-driven trucks to a flour mill where the wheat seeds are ground into flour. This is taken by fossil fuel-driven trucks to the baker.

Fossil fuels are used to cook up a mixture of flour, water, butter and sugar into cookies. Carbon dioxide is released when cookies are heated.

Cookies are then taken to the supermarket in a fossil fuel-driven truck and you travel to the supermarket in a fossil fuel-driven car to buy cookies.

Without fossil fuels there would be no food from farms. No cookies.

All food is carbon-based. Our bodies contain carbon. Our bodies recycle carbon. Without carbon, we die. Cookies are rich in carbon. This carbon is used by the body and is not poisonous. If you eat far too many cookies, you may vomit. Serves you right!

Far too many cookies?

If we eat a cookie and wash it down with a soda, cola or water, the body changes the cookie. Saliva starts to break down the food and messages are sent to the stomach to prepare to use the chewed cookie.

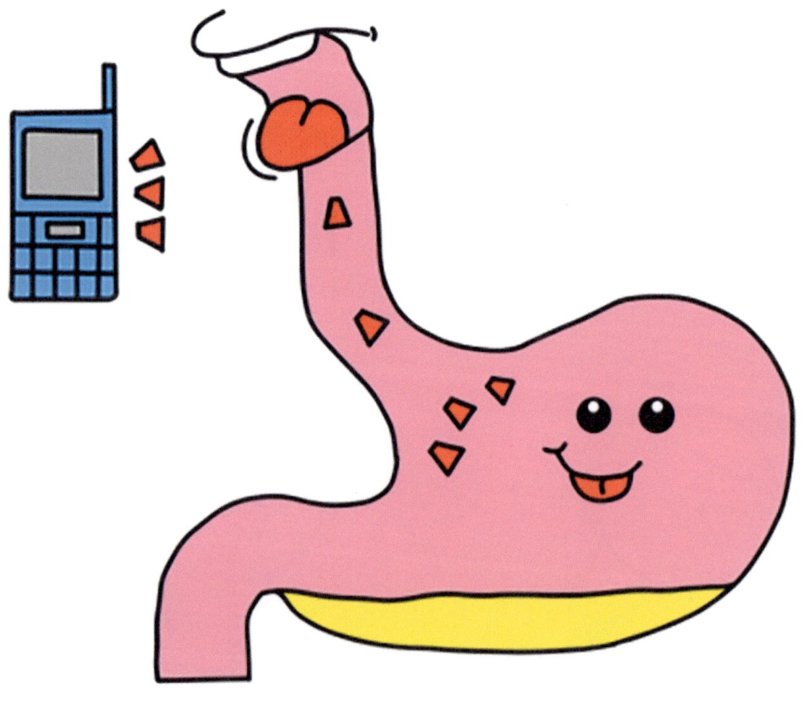

When the chewed cookie is in the stomach, bacteria and chemicals in your stomach break the food down, useful carbon-rich materials enter the blood stream and waste is removed as poo, wee and farts.

Most of the carbon-rich materials are sugars, they keep the brain working, give energy to muscles, replace dead cells and add new cells as you grow up. Without sugars, the brain can live on fats.

Without sugar or fats, you end up pushing up daisies.

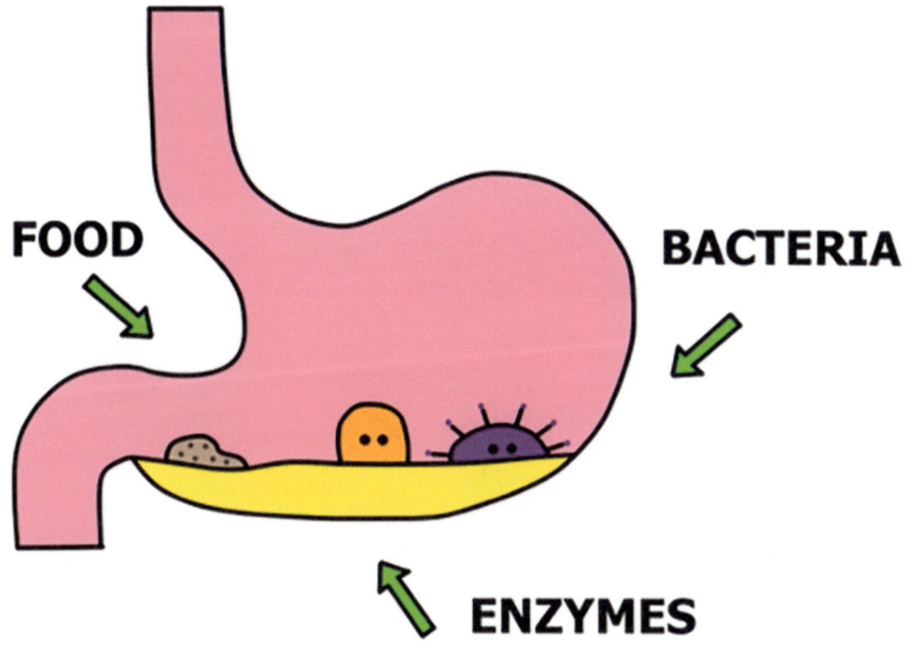

Human wee is mostly water plus chemical wastes from your muscles and kidneys. Your kidneys filter out waste materials from your blood and add them to urine. Most of these chemical wastes contain carbon.

SCIENTIFIC EXPERIMENT FOR BOYS

Find a private place and wee on the same plant as many times you can over a period of a few months. Will the plant grow or die? Do the experiment.

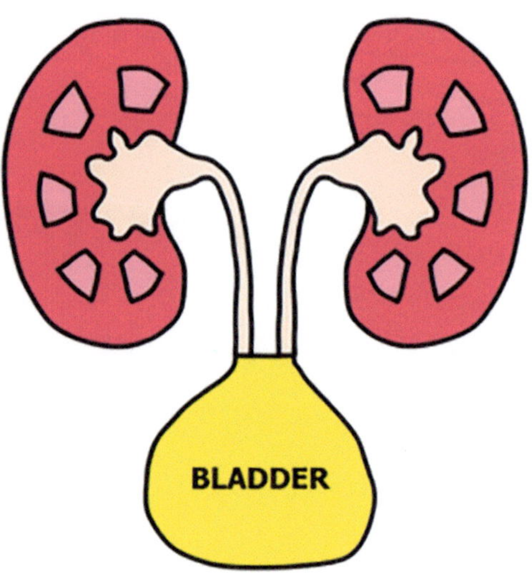

When explorers in the desert ran out of water, they drank their own wee so they didn't die of thirst. Yuk. Drinking wee did not kill them. Don't try this at home. Or in the desert. Or at school. Or anywhere.

DID YOU KNOW?

Wee is yellow because of chemicals formed when blood breaks down into waste products. Wee should be colourless. If your wee is yellow, drink more water.

Wee is one way of getting rid of the carbon-rich waste products from your body after eating cookies and drinking.

Poo or die!

Poo is another way. If you don't eat, you don't poo. If you don't poo, you die.

Most of poo is water. The rest is carbon chemicals, undigested materials and all sorts of dangerous germs.

A teaspoon full of poo contains 50 million viruses, 5 million bacteria, 5,000 parasite cysts and 500 parasite eggs. Don't eat poo. Go hungry instead.

Hundreds of years ago, people used spoons made from bone or wood. Germs were in the cracks and holes and often killed people.

Later, spoons were made of expensive pewter, bronze or silver. There were no cracks to hide germs and the germs were killed by the metals.

It took thousands of years of invention before the modern cheap stainless steel spoon appeared. It has no cracks for germs.

To make a spoon such that you won't be poisoned by metals or germs, rocks rich in iron need to be mined using energy, transported to a port using energy, carried by ships using energy to a smelter that uses energy and coal is used to change iron-rich rocks to iron.

Stainless steel also has chromium and nickel which must be mined, transported and smelted using coal and energy. Very hot molten iron is mixed with molten chromium and molten nickel to make stainless steel.

If we stop using coal or ban mining, we go back to past times when just to use a spoon made of bone or wood could be a death sentence. Please don't die. You can use energy, metals and coal and not make a mess of the planet.

Poo can be poisonous. This is why we wash our hands after the bathroom.

About 700 million poor people in the world have no toilets. They poo outside wherever they can. This is a larger environmental problem than climate change. It leads to disease and death, especially of children your age.

Human poo is very different from cow poo. You have a small and large intestine in your stomach. Cows have four stomachs, each of which has a different job.

For hundreds of years, humans have used their own poo and wee as fertiliser for plants. Poo contains dangerous germs and traces of metal poisons. Leaf vegetables fertilised with poo often causes serious sickness.

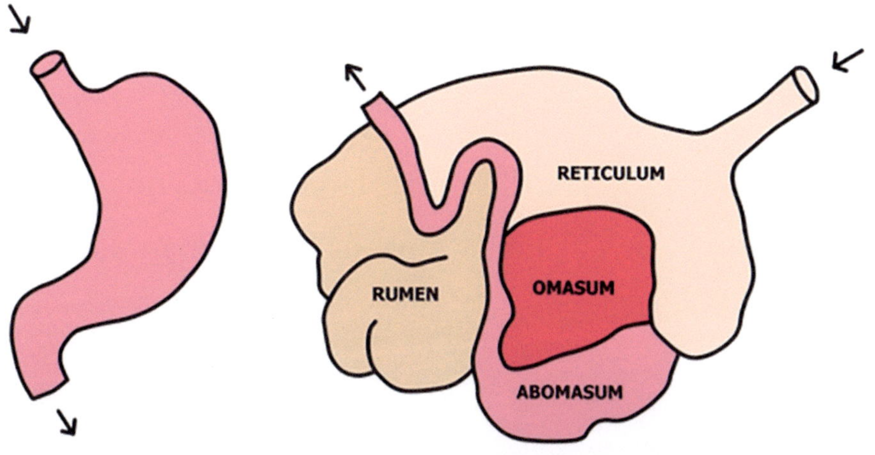

SCIENTIFIC EXPERIMENT

Cows eat grass and convert it to energy. Humans can't because we don't have four stomachs. Try it. Collect some grass, wash and eat. Check your poo later and you will see bits of green grass because you cannot use grass. Dogs eat grass when they need fibre.

This is why we now make fertilisers in factories using gas. Plants grow far bigger and better using factory fertilisers than from poo fertiliser.

Cow poo is a good fertiliser for plants. It does not contain dangerous germs or metal poisons like human poo.

As cow poo breaks down, it gives out heat. Check it out. If you can find a pile of cow poo, put your hand in it. The poo will be warm. Will you wash your hands after the cow poo test?

For hundreds of years people used poo, twigs and leaves for cooking and heating fires in huts.

About 2 billion people still do because they have no cheap electricity made from coal.

Children and their mothers die from the fumes from burning cow poo. That's not fair.

Coal burned to make electricity brought people out of poverty and saved lives.

When there is electricity, children can do homework, food can be kept fresh in fridges, food can be cooked and homes can be heated and cooled.

Many people in the world use polluted water from wells and rivers for drinking, cooking and washing. Germs in the water kill people, especially children like you. Is that fair?

With cheap constant electricity made from burning coal, water can be pumped from dams and bores to houses and germs in water can be killed.

Electricity generated from wind and solar machines is too expensive and unreliable whether you are rich or poor. No electricity is generated when there is no wind or when the Sun does not shine at night.

If poor people have no electricity made from coal, then they die.

Humans get rid of about 1 kg of waste as poo, wee and farts every day. Elephants release about 40 kg a day. Large dinosaurs would have released even more.

Some scientists study fossilised poo called coprolites. Will you become a coprolite expert?

Archaeologists have found clay tablets with fart jokes written on them. The tablets are 4,000 years old.

Not all farts smell. Loud farts are because of strong stomach muscles. Don't try to fart loudly if you have a belly ache.

Dogs and cats fart silently because they have no bum or butt cheeks. Some dog farts are silent and deadly.

Experienced dog farters get up and slowly walk away leaving their owners with the stink.

Dogs know exactly what they are doing.

If you try to stop a fart, the gas stays in your guts, gets into your blood, is released into your lungs and you breathe out a rotten smell. Better to let one rip rather than have a fart do another lap through your body and come out your mouth.

Let one rip!

Digestion of cookies and soda or cola produces solids (poo), liquids (wee) and gas (farts). All contain carbon chemicals that come from the carbon rich food you eat. Without carbon you are dead.

Farts mainly contain nitrogen, oxygen, hydrogen, carbon dioxide and methane. Smelly farts contain rotten egg gas.

DON'T TRY THIS AT HOME

Farts can be lit with a match to produce a blue flame. Lighting farts can burn skin so fart flamers wear pants.

What chemical in farts burns?

If you fart in the bath, bubbles of these gases bubble to the surface. Don't believe me, try it and try to count the number of bubbles. You'd better be quick.

SCIENTIFIC EXPERIMENT

How do I stink out the whole bus on a school excursion? Eat as many eggs as possible. Eat cabbage. Then wait for the action to start and look at which friend you are going to blame. Some people drop a smelly fart just as the doors of an elevator shut. There is no escape. Don't even try this with friends.

Humans fart about 15 times a day and farts move away from you at more than 10 kilometres per hour. That makes it easy to blame someone else or even the dog. However, say nothing because if you smelt it, you dealt it.

A hundred years ago, the French stage performer Le Pétomane gulped in large amounts of air and then was able to fart long musical tunes to laughing audiences. One of the first sound recordings ever made was by Thomas Edison of Le Pétomane performing his farting music.

If you practised hard like Le Pétomane did, you could fart out a tune by gulping air and controlling your bum muscles. Only try this in front of your grandparents and not at school.

Some farts are silent and deadly.

SCIENTIFIC EXPERIMENT

Count the number of times you fart in a day.

You also fart when asleep.

Are you an A-grade farter with more than 20 farts a day?

Deadly farts are extremely smelly, far worse than rotten egg gas. This is due to carbon chemicals that smell like rotten cabbage. Other very smelly farts have another carbon chemical that smells like rotten seaweed.

Impress your friends when one of them lets go something that would kill an elephant. If there is a rotten cabbage smell tell them it's due to methyl mercaptan, if the smell is like rotten seaweed, tell them it's due to dimethyl sulphide. They will think of you as the school's fart genius.

Sometimes people will say they had a "brain fart" when they did something very silly.

Burps come from swallowing air when eating and drinking. In some cultures, you must burp at the meal table to show you liked the meal.

Each day we release about a litre of gas from burping. If you drink something with bubbles in it like soda or cola, the carbon dioxide in these drinks is released by burping.

Air contains nitrogen and oxygen and traces of other gases such as argon and carbon dioxide. When we breathe in, the body uses the oxygen from air and the waste carbon from food to make carbon dioxide.

We breathe out 100 times more carbon dioxide than we breathe in.

HOW DO YOU KNOW YOU ARE ALIVE?

You breathe out carbon dioxide and your bum points to the ground.

WHAT IS ARSINE?

If you eat a lot of rice and drink rice "milk", you might breathe out the very poisonous smelly gas arsine.

Some people have bad breath. This comes from a dry mouth and 150 different smelly carbon chemicals which are the waste products from bacteria in the mouth.

If you don't want to be kissed by an old aunt or grandparent, chew eggs, onions and garlic for as long as possible. Your breath will stop anyone coming near you.

Ear wax protects skin in the ears and keeps this skin wet. It also has chemicals that fight harmful bacteria. These chemicals are carbon-rich waste.

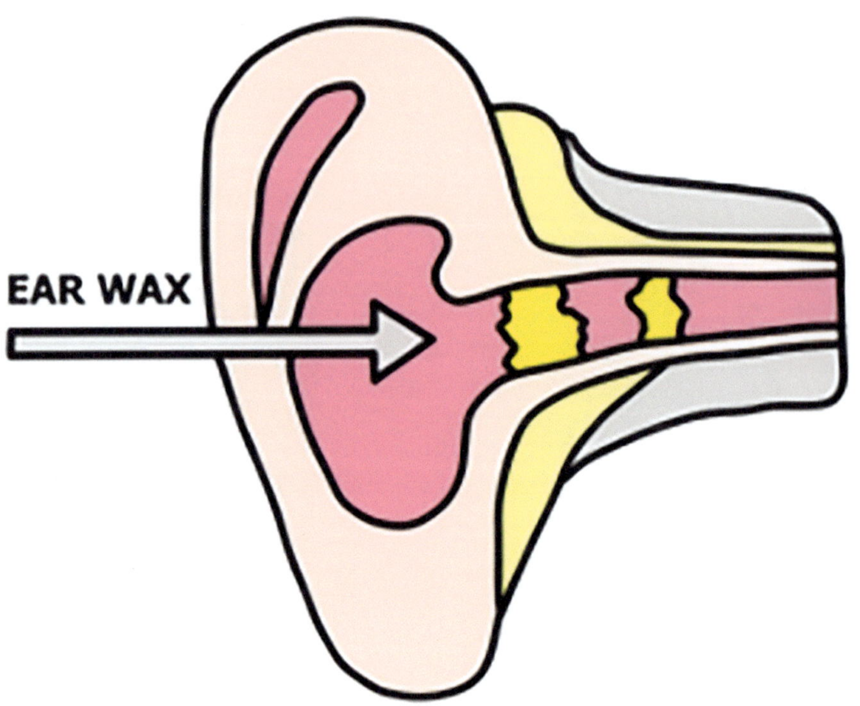

There is a video of a man eating his own ear wax in the Australian parliament. Yuk. He later became Australia's prime minister. Could you become Prime Minister if you eat ear wax in public? Do an internet search using the key words *Rudd ear wax eat.*

Boogers are also waste. They start life as mucus or snot which contain carbon chemicals and salt waste.

Boogers contain germs and if you pick your nose too many times, it can bleed.

SOMETHING SALTY?

When you eat a booger, the taste is due to salt.

Tiny wet hairs inside your nose catch dust, pollen and bacteria in the air you breathe in before the air goes into your lungs. If you live in a dusty place, you will have more boogers. The colour of your booger depends on the colour of the dust.

When you have a cold, your body makes extra mucus to protect your body.

If you have snot and boogers, your body is healthy. It is getting rid of waste and catching small particles that should not go into your lungs.

HEALTH WARNING

If you pick your nose too hard, your head might cave in.

Your body takes carbon from food and converts it to many carbon chemicals. Some carbon chemicals are used for growing, others end up in waste in wee, poo, farts, ear wax and boogers.

SCIENTIFIC EXPERIMENT

Roll a booger flat and look at it under a microscope. There may be hair and tiny pieces of dust. Each year, 80,000 tonnes of dust falls onto the Earth from outer space. If you are very lucky, you might have a piece of this extra terrestrial dust in your booger. Not many people are lucky enough to have aliens in their boogers.

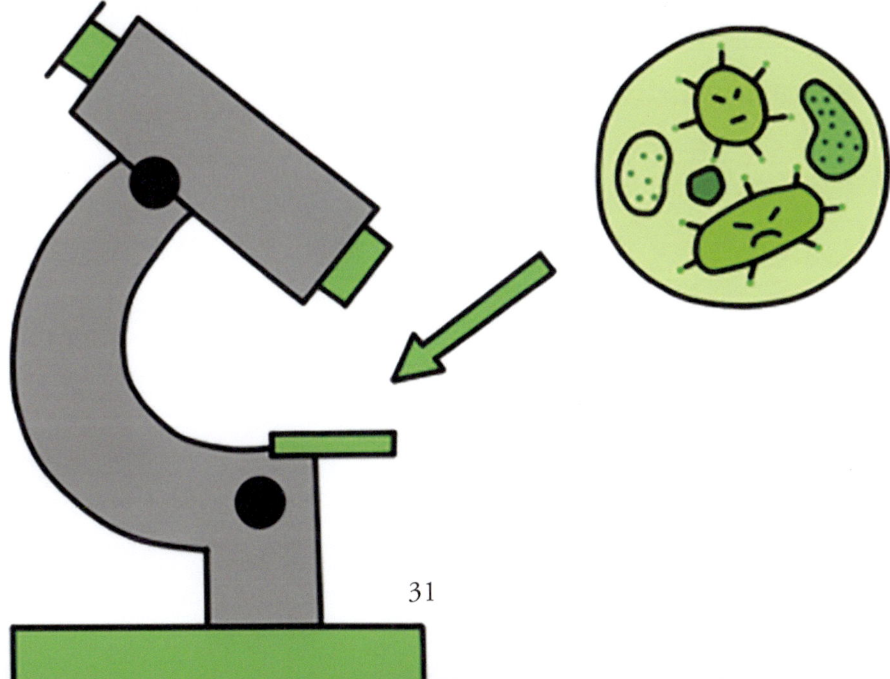

Without carbon, there is no life.

No plants. No animals. No food. No you.

If you think carbon is pollution, stop eating and you will drop dead. Maybe there is no such thing as carbon pollution.

In the past, there was hundreds of times as much carbon dioxide in the air. There was no runaway global warming. In fact, there were ice ages.

Reefs grew faster and larger and the oceans didn't become acid. Maybe much of what you hear about climate change is to scare you.

Hundreds of years ago, most trees in Europe, America and England were chopped down and burned to make charcoal used to make iron and glass. Charcoal was also used for heating and cooking.

It was discovered that coal could do a better job for making iron, glass and heating, so forests were not chopped down and started to regenerate. The use of coal, a fossil fuel, saved the forests of Europe, America and England.

Whale oil had been used for hundreds of years. It was burned in lanterns as there was no electricity then for lights.

About 150 years ago, fossil fuel oil started to be used for lanterns. Whales were then not killed for oil. It was fossil fuel that saved the whales.

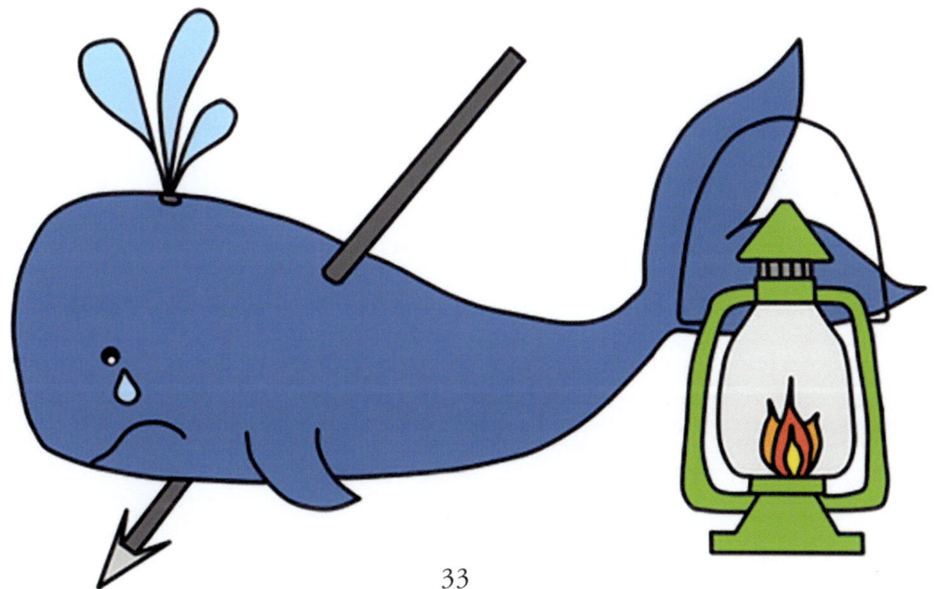

About 150 years ago, streets had piles of horse poo. Cities were environmental disasters. People became sick and died from the bacteria and viruses in the poo, especially when the poo washed into water wells.

As soon as fossil fuel cars were invented, cities had almost no horse poo. Fossil-fuel driven cars saved the lives many city people.

Carbon is everywhere. In the air. In rocks. In the sea. In your food. In your wee, poo, farts, burps, breath, boogers and ear wax.

For thousands of years, people have been telling stories which may not be true just to scare us and so they can be the centre of attention.

No one has proven that carbon released by humans changes climate. You are told that there is carbon pollution to make you anxious and fearful and to make the story-teller feel important and the centre of attention.

Without carbon there is no food and no life. If you are told that carbon pollution is bad, tell the story teller to lead by example and drop dead because food is carbon rich.

Humans live in the mountains, by the sea, on the ice, in the tropics, in deserts and in warm wet climates. Humans have already adapted to live in all climates.

There is more carbon dioxide used as plant food on planet Earth than is emitted by humans. The rest of carbon dioxide comes from the oceans.

The more carbon dioxide in the air, the better it is for plants. Scientists are yet to show that human emissions of carbon dioxide change climate.

People have been frightening others by saying the world will end soon so they can look important. If just one end of the world prediction came true, you wouldn't be here. Nor would your parents, grandparents or any other person.

The planet has been around for 4,567 million years. Climate has always changed and always will. The temperature is the same as it was 50 years ago. The temperature now is cooler than 5,000, 50,000 or 50 million years ago.

How can there now be a climate crisis or climate emergency? Unless, of course, someone is telling you stories.

When someone tells you the world will end because of human emissions or a climate crisis, tell them what you think using your very own emissions.

Fart or burp loudly.

For parents and grandparents

We are all environmentalists. We want a better planet for ourselves and future generations. We do not want to be manipulated, told lies or be bombarded with exaggerated hysteria about the state of the planet. In my life of more than three score and ten years, the planet in my neck of the woods has got better because of greater wealth, technology and environmental awareness.

I have seen a huge improvement in air, water and soil quality; a change from reusing everything because of poverty to recycling; better, more efficient and cheaper consumables and cars; better, more diverse and cheaper food; better health and greater longevity; more disposable cash and the ability to travel cheaply with ease to places we could only dream about when I was young. The streets are no longer used as effluent drains and places to dump rubbish.

In my lifetime, I have seen the appearance of plumbing systems for water and sewage, extensive public transport, sealed roads and cheap reliable employment-generating electricity. As we became wealthier and wealthier, we used more and more energy and polluted less. As children, we couldn't wait to be an adult in the new modern world and there was no such thing as ecoanxiety.

This book is for parents and grandparents to read and show to children. Maybe children will also read the book. It is hard for children to escape from the clutches of incessant negative emotionally-disturbing propaganda that they receive at school regarding the health of the planet. This brain washing propaganda exploits vulnerability and is easily recognised by jargon, disorganised phrases, negativity and a lack of logic. It is an attempt to change the world into a place with serfs controlled by unelected elites. It's time to deprogram children and hit the reset button. Schools have now become the playgrounds for activists and weirdos promoting an unhealthy view of the family, gender, sex and science. Children should be learning about the history of our planet.

School should be fun with young people given the basics for survival in later life and places where young people are taught to question, think critically and analytically and commit a large body of knowledge to memory. The social, ethical, political and religious ideas should be moulded at home in a family setting. However, this is becoming increasingly difficult because, in many western countries, the extended family structure has broken down and children become ripe for the picking by cult-like figures. Education is for life and should produce self-sufficient citizens.

We spend our lives dealing with snake oil salesmen trying to con us so children need to be able to argue, see the fallacy of bland statements and meaningless chants and know how to ask incisive questions such as

"Show me the evidence?" Children need to be trained to spot snake oil at 100 paces.

If a child "Googles it" or uses Wikipedia, then they can be exposed to a body of corrupted biased selective information that is often demonstrably wrong. They are certainly not gaining knowledge using a search engine. This book provides a few uncomfortable and obscure facts, asks questions that children should be asking and exposes children to the thread that underpins all science: scepticism.

As a parent and grandparent, I enjoyed the evolution, learning, achievements and interaction of the little ones. I have had much help from many parents, grandparents, children and grandchildren in trying to convey the ideas in this book. It is hard to tell children that their teachers are ignorant activists with no interest in the nation or children's futures; that their teachers obfuscate and distort fundamental science, the environment and history; that they are victims of the left's successful great march through the education system and that a so-called education has not provided children with basic knowledge and the skills to criticise, analyse and argue. It is time to save the children from nonsense.

The author often gets accused of being controversial. If being controversial is to tell the truth, use validated facts and be sceptical of everything, then so be it.

Ian Plimer's Books

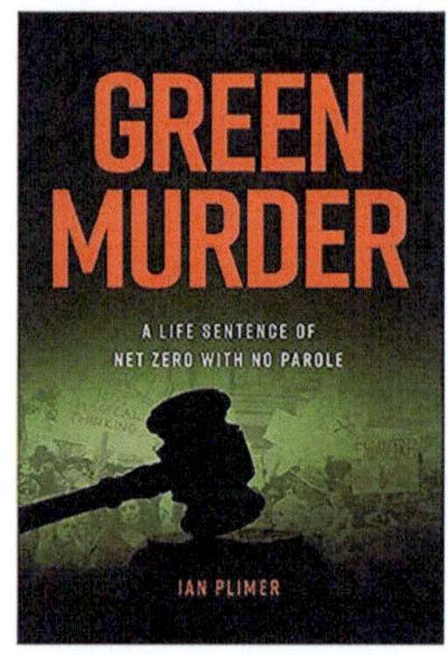

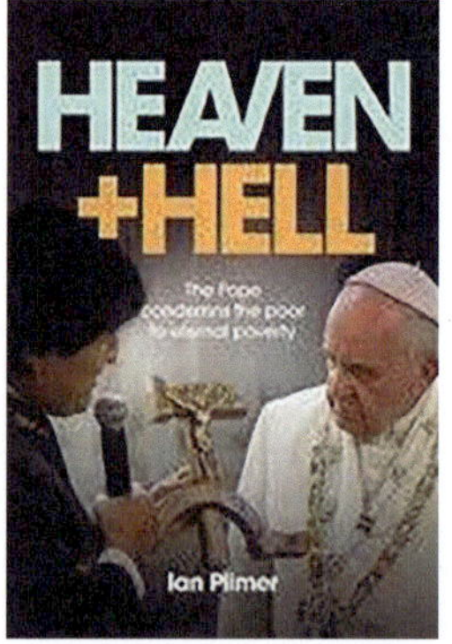